# WINDFALLS

## Poems by
## John Mash

**Windfalls**

ISBN: 978-1-907540-27-1

Printed by BookPrintingOnline.co.uk

Published by
Anchorprint Group Limited
December 2010

Reprinted 2015

# Author's Foreword

This book represents a good deal of what I have sought to put into verse over the past fifty years or more. It is roughly grouped into sections, on faith and religion, on vaguely humorous topics at times reflecting my more cynical side, and on a number of miscellaneous themes. I have above all sought variety – variety in rhythms and verse patterns, variety between rhyme and blank verse.

My intention is to give the reader some food for thought, an occasional smile, and perhaps an inkling of the Christian faith that underlines my writing.

I would like to thank my family and friends who have helped me along the way, and particularly my friend Timothy Lewis who suggested the book and has encouraged me throughout.

I hope that you, the reader, will enjoy the poems, and find my book worthwhile dipping into now and then.

John Mash

# OF CABBAGES
# AND
# KINGS

## FIRST KISS

That first kiss
Was salty, unexpected,
Standing just apart,
Under the dripping winter trees.

I heard my heart beat loud
As I bent forward –
So careful;
And she looked up at me
Unsmiling, beautiful,
And turned her face
Ever so slightly upward.

For an eternity we stood
While the rain poured down
Haloed in the street lamp,
Our eyes locked together.
And then somehow, we kissed –
Her mouth on mine,
As soft as rabbit's foot.

That was all.  I said goodnight
Ran over to my bike, and waved,
And cycled home on air.

# FINNINGHAM

Shall I return again

To the land of sugar beet and horse-drawn ploughs,
And cider apples, glossy red on groaning boughs,
And limpid streams meandering through the fen,
And high-pitched brogue of honest Suffolk men?


And shall I hear once more

The patient swishing of sleek guernseys' tails,
The soft squirting of fresh milk into pails,
The jangling jumping bell of the village store,
And buzz of village gossip filtering through the door?


If I go back, shall I find

The East wind blowing blithely on her face,
Imbuing it with such healthy lively grace?
Will she still be cycling along the winding road
Bearing home-made basket brimming with home-baked load?


Alas, no more for me those days:

I have changed now.  I am distant and old.
And the village has changed - commerce has taken hold.
We would not know each other, our eyes would glaze:
Only in dreams can I retread former ways.

## COULD I RELIVE...

In fretful wakefulness I lie
As today becomes tomorrow;
I dare not give myself to sleep:
My dreams bring too much sorrow.

Out of my eyes my anguish pours,
No relief to my remorse:
Could I relive that single hour -
Of all my pain the source.

It's not enough to say "Repent!
In time the memory will relent;
Stand up and live once more."
My mind obeys, but in my heart
The knife still turns, the wound still smarts -
The lifeblood beats no more.

## FAR FAR AWAY...

Far far away
In the camel's eye,
In the peacock's train,
In the parakeet's sheen,
Is the lust of youth
And what might have been.

Into the air
With a puff of wind,
Like a grain of the desert
Falling in rain,
Is the old desire
Now turned to pain.

The lavender smell
Of the sun-kissed fields,
The gossamer trace
Of the spider's lair,
Is my recollection
Of her hair.

Ah! the warmth of the sun
Caressing our limbs,
Confirming our youth
As we intertwined
Remains but a shadow
Crossing the mind.

The years gather in
With a uniform grey.
As I nod by the fire
And gaze at the rain,
I unlock my dreams
And grow young again.

# CHINTHURST HILL

A horse in a buttercup meadow,
A chestnut in summer array,
A skyline suffused with faint greenness,
Are what I walk out to each day.

As I climb up the shadowy pathway,
The tower at the top of the hill
Pokes its head above neighbouring bushes
And waits for me, silent and still.

The doors are now boarded with plywood,
The battlements broken and skew,
The appearance of age a deception,
It's twentieth century, new.

And along from the tower, an oak tree
Horizontally spreads on the ground,
Where small children hide from their fathers
And earnestly hope to be found.

Their laughter rings out on the hilltop,
Their voices and footsteps grow faint,
As I take up my place on the tree trunk,
And meditate idly, or paint.

The sun drags the shadows across me,
As it disappears over the brow;
But I linger, still wrapped in the calmness:
All is silence and solitude now.

At last I concede to the darkness,
And carefully thread my path down
To the house, which is right by the meadow
With the horse, and the buttercup gown.

I stop at the edge of the garden,
To feel for the gate-catch release;
And I cast a look backward to Chinthurst -
The hill where my heart has found peace.

## FULL MOON

A new beauty has the moon tonight -
Recreated in perpetuity;
The orb beyond the fingertips,
The apple of paradise,
Suspended in grace.


The limbs have lost their sheen,
The eyes their youthful spark,
The lids lie heavy with years.
The spring of the heels is worn weak,
The mind, less nimble, runs no longer
But walks from thought to thought;
And time marks one more notch.


But lady moon moves slowly on,
Spanning her ocean of sky,
Timeless in human time.

## IN POPPY FIELDS

The hunger shines out through her pleading eyes:
How can I satisfy that mute desire?
The love that binds us once was fierce enough
In poppy fields, when we were both on fire.

But now my seeds are spilt, my petals sere:
A second flowering sparser than the first.
I have no answer to this urgency -
No welling spring to slake such burning thirst.

But as we sit together by the fire,
Talking of children, sharing memories past;
Sometimes a spark ignites my loins again:
And ever so slightly, the old pulse beats fast.

Then among gleanings of remembered years
A few last poppies spread their banners thin:
And as we clasp the old familiar flesh
How eagerly my crop is garnered in.

# ONCE UPON A MOONLIGHT

Once upon a moonlight
In the April years,
Came a girl a-dancing,
Garlands round her ears.
All she wore was nothing
Save her maidenhair:
As I reached she vanished,
Vanished into air.

Stiffly in November,
With her cloak of grise
I turn back to springtime
Through my memories.
Past the summer beaches,
Crowded yet alone -
To the dancing forest
Where her beauty shone.

Nothing can I conjure:
All I see is night
Hanging from the branches,
Curtaining my sight.
Slowly into winter
Shedding icy tears,
Empty pain I carry
From the April years.

## SISYPHUS

"Bother!" said Sisyphus in Greek,
As he watched his rolling stone
Gathering no satisfaction,
Skeltering down to the bottom of old Tartarus.
"Bother" he said, for the millionth time -
Then noticed me.

"Sisyphus, Sisyphus," I said,
"Why despair?
Toss yourself again into the throes of time.
When eternity is over, then
You shall achieve your desire.
Then all you seek shall be set like a crown
On the mountain top,
And you shall be shriven and clean.

My name is Sisyphus too -
And every day and every day
I roll my fantasies on.
Sometimes the stars escape me
And trampled dust is all I see.
But reaching out, I go -
Grasping the upper air
Only to see my stone topple
And hurtle into fragments."

"This is hell," said Tantalus,
Reaching for the grapes in wrath.
"Though I realise and recognise
The Alpha and Omega of absolute denial,
All my senses say: 'desire, desire'."
Weeping he turned - and noticed me.

"O Tantalus, I understand,
I understand," I said, and hurried on -
I was weeping too.

## POLZEATH

The waves echo in the cavern;
The light runs along the wall in ripples,
The seeming solid shimmers with motion
Perpetually, unceasingly, as I gaze.


The rock dissolves in spray, and re-appears,
And renews the conflict shining wet,
And vanishes again and re-emerges.
Such firmness, yet such futility.
Water weaves rock into her own designs patiently.


My days are brief, my moments seconds,
My everlasting flesh, my essence,
All an ephemeral vision,
Battered by time,
Changing imperceptibly
Into a coffin-shaped old age.

## PENELOPE

When Ulysses came striding home,
Sweeping aside the suitors,
He took his wife in the weather-beaten arms
That had once dealt death to Trojans
And embraced the fair Calypso on a foreign strand,
And kissed her tenderly.


"O dear one," she said, "all these years
I have waited, I have woven, I have spun,
I have nurtured your child Telemachus,
I have been faithful, I have hoped."


Ulysses looked into her worn eyes,
At the face wrinkled with half-despair
Of nineteen years, at the hands
Calloused from the loom
At the hair, wispy, without lustre,
At the breasts no longer firm against his chest:


"O dear one," he said,
"You are beautiful still, and I love you."

## STARLINGS

Clockwork starlings on the lawn,
Strutting stiffly to and fro;
Jerking animated heads
Bright with lustrous glow.


Pecking, preening, all day long;
Cleaning quills with awkward pride;
Deploying individual feet
Maudlin from side to side.


Opening, shutting ugly beaks,
Showing shell-pink hue within;
Squawking tuneless noisy sounds -
Companionable din.

## THE RIVALS

As I recall the happy days
When we were young together,
I see you with my inward eye
Skipping through the heather.

Virile you were, and debonair,
With locks both long and thick;
And I recall my jealousy:
My God, you made me sick.

For you were all I longed to be;
The girls, they loved you only.
My hated, envied rival, yes –
But now you're dead.  And me? I guess
I feel a little lonely.

## WATERCOLOUR MEN

If we could only live oil painting lives,
How graphically simple it would be
To touch up each unfolding scene,
Overlaying brightness on misery;
Using today's brand new palette knife
To rectify errors of earlier days,
Or even to scrape the canvas clean
And paint new beauty on last year's greys.


Alas, we are all watercolour men:
Too fragile the texture of our paper lives
To smudge out ill-fitting colours and tones
With our repentant brushes and knives.
Too often, to our infinite regret,
The picture is fixed in colours fast.
But occasionally, when the light shines through,
We are not dissatisfied with pictures past.

# THERE IS ONLY GROWING OLD

There is only growing old:
Like a tree
Spreadeagled once,
Over the ground that nourished it;
Now a dry gnarled finger
Pointing up at the sky,
Issuing a hopeless challenge
To the years.

There is only growing old:
Like a citadel
In the Italian hills,
Strong once, against all comers,
Embracing the fearful townsfolk,
Girding them round like a sheepfold;
Now desolate
Eroded by the timeless winds
Grain by grain -
No future, only a forgotten past,
Drowned in the memories of men
Long since buried by their sons.


There is only growing old:
Like a painting:
Wrought by a Flemish master,
Once bright, startling the eye
With colours fresh, alive;
Now gathering molecules of grime,
Opening fissures in faces,
Hairlines in hands -
A fading remembrancer of past years.

There is only growing old:
Like a star,
Once shimmering, piercing the sky
With white hot light;
Now dull, reflective, waning
As it drifts in its eternal orbit.

There is only growing old.


## WHITESANDS BAY

Why, when I see the breaking of a wave
Caught in brief sunlight on a bleak Welsh shore,
Does the old hopeless longing come again?
Why does my joy leave me sadder than before?


It is the very sameness of the past -
The constant washing of the years that I regret -
Wearing away the edges of the soul:
Only during calm seas can I forget.


Is it the calm, or numbing of the sense,
That frees me from the handcuffs of recall?
No matter:  I walk steadily ahead
Until I drown in the stillest sea of all.

## THE SOLENT

One pull of the navel cord
Bringing to birth the engine's roar:
The whiff of petrol, salty-soaring spray
That follows us from the sea shore;
The insubstantial motion
Tossed and ship-slapped on fretting side
Makes for a bottomless pit in the belly
And an inward ebb and flow of tide.


One inch from sea-green death below,
A narrow timber bulwark takes the strain;
The motor spumes defiant smoke
And thrashes the angry waters in its train.
Such buoyant power, joyous in its risk -
At the heart of man lurks such desire:
To strive nearer the devil-dancing flames -
Only the luckless fall screaming into the fire.


One thrust of the helm, and we are nosing back;
The comfortable browns and greens reappear.
Into focus leaps the lens of the land,
And each wave lessens the unspoken fear.
We loved each minute, would not have stayed
At the water's edge;  but glistening wet
We halter our sea-horse at the quay:
Our relief outmatches twinges of regret.

# THE AGORAPHOBE

I keep the curtains drawn
The light bulb is my sun -
The wireless is my company,
It's all my friends in one.


I hear the traffic roar,
The footsteps hurrying by;
They cannot reach me, I am safe:
The ceiling is my sky.


My outdoors is the lounge,
My indoors is my bed.
The hall a dangerous passageway
Where visitors may tread.


I settle by the fire,
The firewood spits and sings:
I come alive on winter eves,
And spread my timid wings.


Here I keep death at bay;
These walls are all I crave.
The open window is my death,
The outside world, my grave.

## THE ENGAGEMENT

Are you really going to marry him, my dear?
Are you going to trot up the aisle
With snuffling page boys, and weepy mothers,
And dozens of irritable relations -
Itching in pins and petticoats,
In pinstripes and sweaty frock-coats,
Wondering where on earth to put their top hats,
Faces cracking with continuous smile?


Listen how he blows his nose, my dear:
Hark how he drowns his lips in the soup.
Spy out the secret shaving soap behind his ears.
Tell out the continual tattoo of his pipe-dirty fingers,
On clean face-polished furniture,
And think: "All mine to have and behold."


I married a man long years ago, my dear.
Fair he was, and clean.
I loved to lie with him in the grass in the sun in the park,
And pile green clovers on his eyelids,
And kiss them off again, and start anew.
I loved to lie with him.


But now he sits in the garden,
Quivering with snores,
Bronzing his big belly in the sun -
And oh! I am lonely with him.

## THE INVIGILATOR

The scraping and scuffling of shoes,
The deep impression of desperate pen on paper,
The furious screwing up of scripts
Irredeemably spoiled,
The vacant staring at the hands
Of the remorseless clock:
These are the marks of the doomed,
Convinced of their own inadequacies,
Lost in a desert of words.

And here and there an oasis:
One or two quiet boys writing,
Oblivious of all save their muse,
Scribbling their ultimate solution
To the question that has vexed generations.

One such was far into his private world
Until the final summons came.
Then hastily stopped, stretched,
Collected his effects, and walked out quietly.
Alongside, his relieved and chattering peers
Returned to normalcy.

I marked his script: it was the worst of all.
The top marks went to a scuffler
Who had not sat still
For two minutes together.
He will go far, an alert and original mind.
But I think the other will live more happily.

# FELIXSTOWE FERRY

Lying in the long grass,
Bodies pressed together;
Listening to the lapping waves,
Smelling the sweet heather.


Overhead the seagulls,
In front of us the sea;
Behind, the sea wall's shelter -
And here, just her and me.


I loved her, yet I left her,
And tore her heart away.
A deadly serious game was that -
Not just a childish play.


Oh! That she would return to me.
Oh! That we'd lie again
In the smooth summer grasses
Of that quiet Suffolk fen.

## DENTS DU MIDI

The mountains sleep
Cloaked in a rosy mist;
And all the plain far, far below
With softest touch of dew is kissed.


The quiet of dawn,
Still sunless on the peaks,
Is but a prelude to the day -
The hush before the poet speaks.


My spirit rests,
Soundless and calm and dumb;
Yet when the sun expands his rays
I know that searing pains will come.


Sunrise, be still!
Mountains, hold back the morn!
Then may my heart forever rest
In a perpetual painless dawn.

## LOVE UNREQUITED

The oak upholds his limbs in scorn
And cares not if I be forlorn:
For he has seen the years unfold,
And concentrates on growing old.


The elm, round whom the ivy creeps,
Is satisfied with love, and sleeps:
Deaf are his gnarled and aged ears
To lovers' plaints, and lovers' fears.


The birch plays with the wind all day,
And sets her leaves in disarray -
So wrapped in her own fantasy
She has no time to spare for me.


The pine, decked out in olive green,
My melancholy has not seen:
But in the sun her scent distils
To happier lovers in the hills.


But there's a little stream I know,
And thither will I sadly go;
For on its bank there stands a tree
Who weeps and weeps to pity me.

# MIDDLE AGE

I'm over sixty now,
And comfortable, and grey;
And as I sit beside the fire
I sift the embers of desire
From which the flames have long since cooled
And faded far away.

The years of might-have-been
Surround me with their shrouds.
The faces, once so sunny bright,
Now hidden from my groping sight
Still pass me by in waking dreams
Like insubstantial clouds.

I bend to stir the grate:
The coals spit out more light.
One face I seem to recognise -
That kindly smile, those gentle eyes,
Caress my heart as once before,
Then vanish from my sight.

And just across the hearth
Today, as every day,
Sits one who gave her years to me:
The mother of our family.
Her feet are almost touching mine -
A million miles away.

## HOMESICKNESS

Eyes of such darting pain, o'er spilling
Tears so unbidden and unwilling,
As he sits on the edge of the old gnarled chair.
Behind him the bracket clock ticks off
Hour-long minutes, adding to his life
And to his exile in an alien place.


Each signal alerts him to a new distress:
The flickering flames, but from another's hearth,
The nuzzling dog, a friendly stranger only,
The kindly voice, yet not his father's timbre.


We cannot reach him in his cocoon of grief,
Spun by innumerable threads of tender memory.
Only at home will he creep out
And spread his wings of happiness once more.

## PEPPERPOT HIGH

Shall I ever see elves again -
Pepperpot high,
Dancing on the breakfast table?

They were there when I was a little lad,
I spoke with them,
And they shared my cornflakes.
But now the table is bare,
Save for the humdrum stuff of households.

Will the giant ever haunt me again?
Will I ever hear his scraping under the bed,
See his shadow on the wall,
And beg for a night light
To keep him at bay?

Today I still wrestle with giants:
But I cannot see their faces;
And the night light is of no avail.

Shall I ever find the magic forest again?
Where I used to see caves in the bracken,
Waterfalls among the roots of trees,
And cities in the long grasses.

The cities are crumbling now,
Hemmed in by unfinished projects,
And I live in an ungreen wasteland.

O magic forest, where are you now?
O elves, pepperpot high -
Come back and dance once more,
Shadowy giant, hide under the bed again.
Strangely, I miss you.

## THE WEDDING

It wasn't at all how I'd imagined it;
No struggling into age-old morning dress
Smelling of mothballs;
No sharply scripted wedding invitation
Gracing the mantelpiece;
No ancient flinted church with musty smell
And rigid uncompromising pews;
No wedding bells proclaiming from on high
The nuptial ties concluded.


It was an age ago, I know,
When we, his parents married:
And every last detail powerfully planned
According to the whim of the bride's mother.
Even the garden stood to attention at her behest,
Planted in strictly ordered rows
With blooming times precisely governed.
As bride and groom we loved each other,
Promised each other life-long obedience -
That is, after our dues were paid to Her.


Why then my wistfulness, that my own issue
Had struck out such an independent path?
Ah, that was all before the event.
What I will cherish and recall is this:
Two adults making vows of precious worth,
No socially conforming pantomime – but undying love and trust
Shining from their eyes fixed each to each.
And clamouring music importuning heaven  to bless their union.

Singers, composers, pouring out their love,
Surrounding them with their own benison.
And worship rising from the throng,
And friendship leavened with the love of God.
Such a glad procession down the church,
And an unexpected swell of tears within me,
I would not have had it different now.

## THE NIGHT BIRD

Out of the darkness the owl swooped,
Noiseless, beautiful, lithe,
Claws poised -

And the little mouse scurrying home
Looked upwards just in time to see
But not to escape -
And screaming was lifted away
Into the darkness for ever.

# I WALKED THROUGH THE TREES

I walked through the trees
Along a golden gravel path,
And all around, the bubble of spring
Was swelling, swelling, waiting to burst
At the first prick of the sun.

I heard the sap rising, like the music of spheres;
I smelt the fragrant crocus shoots
As they emerged new born
From the soft brown womb of the earth.

I looked up at the tracery of trees
And saw the purple branches
As they shook into green
On the wings of the light March winds.

And I saw an old woman stiffly bend
And pick up a broken twig,
Clutching her brown coat closer.
There stalked autumn, side by side with spring –
And in the shadows behind
The threat of a marble-white winter.

# GRANTCHESTER

We walked to Grantchester the other day,
A friend and I;
Treading through puddles and soft grass,
Threading through puddles
Where broken tresses of ice
Lay steaming in the sun.

Through the kissing gate,
Following three runners -
Bare muddy thighs -
And two little girls,
Laughing over their smooth faces.
Mind that bike! - that infernal
Cacophonal machine,
With its loose mudguard
And George Orwell number plate.

On and on into the western afternoon,
Past cosy teashops, with dumpy faces
Flirting through the oldy window panes,
Tidying dull brown hair with cold red hands,
Waiting for some student's faltering approaches.

And back again,
And through the kissing gate again,
Short-creaking to and  fro;
And back, and back,
To prefaces and doodled notes,
And china tea in earthenware pots,
And fumigas, with the draught under the door.

And so we went,
Talking and thinking, but mostly
Dreaming the Tripos away
Behind the winter branches.

# CRASH VICTIM

I sat by his bed and remembered how
He had fumed at the perverseness of the course,
Torn up his card in a bunker,
And in the clubhouse relived all with relish.

His eyes smiled, and brought back to me
The virile appeal and thrust of the man,
Speeding down foreign ski slopes, and at night
Dancing into the hearts of young girls.

His weak hand moved a little in mine,
And I thought of his strength once:
Formidable, without peer in the classroom;
And as a colleague loyal, complaining, just.

Then he spoke, and the tears coursed down;
And I caught a whiff of his incontinence
As the nurse came to bend his knees
According to the hourly ritual.

"They should have let me die," he said.
Looking at him I could not disagree.
He had been too alive, too vital,
To admit this lingering littleness of life.

# IN LIGHTER VEIN

## LINES LAMENTING THE HOUSE OF LORDS' REFORM

Alas, alas, I was conceived
In ducal sheets of finest silk;
Court circulars proclaimed my birth,
A crested bottle held my milk.

My father's father's uncle's sire
Once bed and breakfasted a king:
Surely a fitting circumstance
Hereditary powers to bring.

But now, an end to privilege:
No more on carpets lush to tread;
No more to sup the best Bordeaux,
No more to sleep on benches red.

Alas, alas, now in the shires
We must consign ourselves to fate,
And watch while low born commoners
Use intellect to steer the state.

## ADAM

The old man looked down at his palms.
"These are the hands" he said,
"To do the work my God demands,
Though they be wrinkly red."


He stretched his legs. "These feet," he smiled,
"For service royal are meant;
To run where e'er my Lord commands
Though they be old and bent."


He stroked his aged chin: "This mouth"
He said, "was made to sing
The praises of the Lord above,
Though cracked and harsh its ring."


He put his hand across his heart:
"This will" he said, "is mine.
God can have all the rest of me,
But here I draw the line."

## CHRISTOPHER ROBIN AND POOH

(to be sung)

Little boy sits on the edge of the seat;
Little grey trousers round little pink feet;
Hush, hush, whatever you do -
Christopher Robin is perched on the loo.


One for Daddy - ah, that feels good!
Wasn't it fun when we played in the wood.
One for Mummy - that's even better:
I'm terribly sorry I upset her.


If I open my legs just a little bit more,
I can see the rubber mat on the floor.
I wonder if Nanny has cleaned it tonight -
Whoops! Now she'll have to, and serve her right.


Little boy sits on the edge of the seat;
Little grey trousers round little pink feet;
Hush, hush, whatever you do -
Christopher Robin is perched on the loo.

## HARVEST HYMN

Come ye wealthy people, cheer:
Raise your glass of wine or beer.
All is safely gathered in:
Every packet, every tin.
Sainsbury's and Waitrose stores
Fill my fridge, and no doubt yours.
Eat your heads off, drink your fill –
Just enjoy:  forget the bill.

Web almighty brings our toys –
Phones for girls, ipods for boys;
And there's Amazon dot.co
Where for comforts we may go.
Do we share our wealth?  No fear:
By *our* efforts we are here –
Though for help the poor may plead
We are deaf:  we've all we need.

So the year comes round again
And we sing our glad refrain:
Here's to me and you and ours –
We've no need of godly powers.
We've no need of church bells ringing,
Priests and people joined in singing,
Down the primrose path we go,
Are we happy?  I don't know.

## NATIVITY PLAY

Please, miss don't make me an angel,
Dressed in white and tinsel and things:
Me mum hasn't got enough cardboard
To cut out a great pair o' wings.

I wouldn't mind bein' the landlord
Of the pub in Bethlehem town:
I've learnt how to walk with a stagger
From me dad, when 'e's got a few down.

Last year I was picked as a Wise Man,
But I don't want that part again, ever.
The others just never stopped laughin' -
They all know I'm not very clever.

Most of all, I'd like to be Joseph,
In a bath towel right down to me toes;
Unless, of course, Mary is Sharon
Who never stops pickin' 'er nose.

Most of the others are shepherds,
Or donkeys and cows in the stall.
Only the angels aren't chosen:
I'm tryin' to make meself small.

I KNEW she'd make me an angel!
I hate it!  I wish I was dead!
I'm glad we're not 'aving Christmas next year -
We're doin' Diwali instead.

## THE CAROL SINGERS

Last night we all went carol singing -
Tracy and Sharon and me -
We wanted to earn a few pennies
To buy us a nice Christmas tree.

Last year me dad brought home a good 'un;
It was huge when we stood it upright.
But this year he's still doing porridge -
It turned out he stole it one night.

So we went to the church for some candles.
(I know where they're all kept in store).
While the other two talked to the verger
I was able to nick three or four.

We'd a charity box for the money
With a hole in the top of the lid.
But also - what nobody realised -
A hole in the bottom , well hid.

We got to the very first doorstep,
And started to sing the first verse,
When out rushed a man in pyjamas
And told us to beat it, or worse.

But we went down the whole street that evening:
We weren't going to do it by halves;
And we carried our song sheets and candles
And money box, all wrapped in scarves.

And some gave us mince pies and money,
And greeted us nice with a smile;
And some even asked us to come in
And stand by the fire for a while.

But others just looked through the window
And waved us away from the door.
So we jumped on the plants in their gardens,
To teach 'em what Christmas is for.

When we got home, the box full of money,
And all of us full of mince pies,
We spread out our dosh on the carpet:
It was really a sight for sore eyes.

At first we were going to spend it
On a tree, like I said at the start -
But a funny feeling of Christmas
Came in and got hold of my heart.

So you see, vicar, that's why we've come here:
To pay for the candles we took.
And the rest of the dosh is for Jesus –
There's ten pounds and 50p - look!

# THE PROBUS CLUB

The fourth Thursday's here once again,
And we're busily sipping our beer,
And some of us have forgotten
Exactly why we are here.

Then the call comes "please be seated,"
And we shamble across to our places,
And try to recall the first names
Of those all-too-familiar faces.

Then a humorous grace is said,
Or sometimes a serious one;
And from the rattle of dentures
We know that the lunch has begun.

We relax amid reminiscence
Of exploits during the war;
With some of us almost regretting
We hadn't been born before.

We listen to long tales of prostates,
Cataracts, pace-makers, new hips,
And holidays down in the Algarve
And luxury cruises on ships.

We make short work of the starter,
And manage a generous roast,
Then we struggle to rise to our feet
In time for the loyal toast.

And sometimes a speaker talks to us
For twenty minutes or more,
And some of us listen intently
And others just sit back and snore.

Then it's over, the meeting's adjourned,
And we leave to get on with our lives,
And some go back to their sweethearts
While others go back to their wives.

And so it goes on month by month
Throughout each advancing year
And then we remember: "It's fellowship –
That's exactly why we are here."


## MY AUNT

My aunt has a great big bum with a wiggle.
Wherever she walks she makes folk giggle.
Some line up with their kids along the road,
And laugh as they watch her joggling her load.
"It looks" they say, as they stare at her back,
"Like two big sea lions fighting in a sack."
And some shout after her, rather unkind:
"Big ship ahoy!" and "Avast behind!"

But every day Auntie ignores all the quips
As she walks to the shop for a big bag of chips.

# I COULD HAVE BEEN FAMOUS

I could have been famous,
My statue in the park after I was dead;
A blue plaque over my birthplace,
A best-selling autobiography;
But I could never get out of bed.

I could have been an inventor -
I was bursting with ideas in my head.
I might have saved the world from poverty,
Or devised the ultimate cancer cure
But I could never get out of bed.

I could have got a top honours degree –
The best of all his year, my tutor said
I knew all the answers, was so articulate,
Far ahead of my peers, but on the day –
I forgot to get out of bed.

When I started in business, my boss told me:
"You're certain to go well ahead.
You'll be a tycoon one of these days."
But in fact I was fired, for once too often
I overslept in my bed.

I'm fairly content now, as I grow old –
The state keeps me quite well fed.
Homelessness has its good points,
But it's sometimes cold in this cardboard box –
How I wish I still had a bed.

## TRUE LOVE

"Will you love me when I'm old and grey
      And sitting by the ashy fire?"
"Don't think of that, my dear, today -
      My love will never tire."


"But will you love me when I'm ill,
      And shivering with an aching fever?"
"My dear, you know I always will:
      My love will last forever."


"But if financial ruin comes,
      And ragged poverty pervades....?"
"You can't expect too much, my dear:
      The strongest fancy fades."

# FAITH, CHURCH AND DOUBTS

# LO! HE COMES....

The Day shall come.
I know not when,
But this I know:
That it will come
Or now or then.

And all creation
Shall respond
Each in its way,
When He shall call
From heaven beyond.

And up shall rise
All lifeless things,
And shall proclaim
In ringing tones
The King of Kings.

But men will writhe
And sweat and groan
And curse and swear
That they chose not
To be His own.

And land and sea
Shall heave and sway
With sheer delight
To see their Maker
On that Day.

And beast and fowl
Shall run or fly
To join the triumph
He shall lead,
From far and nigh.

## COMING TO TERMS

"Cancer - incurable" - no other words can clear
So fast the mist of eternity from my gaze:
My timetable, open-ended up to now,
Is rounded down to weeks and months and days.

And yet, I have been dying a little every day
Since the first hour that brought me through the wall
Of my mother's fierce stretching and pain,
When to the world I made my first bewildered call.

And death, I have always known in my deepest heart,
Waiting just out of sight in the wings of my stage,
Was silently rehearsing his brief walk-on part.
Why then this sudden fear, this anguish, this rage?

Has God cheated me of the small change of my years?
Or has he called me early for reward?
Am I ungrateful not to accept this loving gift
As one who always talked of being with his Lord?

Am I not glad to escape wheezing senility
And thin cold blood, and stiffness of old bones?
Should I not praise my Maker for redeeming me
From humankind's extreme and shadowy zones?

And though I'll see not the flowering of my seed,
Their anniversaries, their own begetting,
Yet they are still my immortality -
Their sun rises still, even as mine is setting.

What then?  Whether I scream with rage and stamp,
And weep a river of frustrated tears,
Or quietly still my racing heart with prayer,
What will be, will be:  none can unlock the years.

Or maybe there is just one, who trod this path
From his free will, and out of love for me:
Lord, hold my hand as I go through the valley -
I'm lonely, and a little afraid, you see.


## PAEAN


Sing out, bells of victory;
Drown the cannon's knell!
Fly, patriotic flags, disguise
The forms of those who fell.


Weeping widow, orphan child,
Rejoice!  We've won the war!
Forget you cannot share this hour
With those you loved before.

## EASTER GARDEN

And then there was the angel:
O.K. as angels go, I suppose -
Wings and snowy white and all that -
But more: a sort of super-angel.
And an eerie noise, like wind through wires,
And a shaking and a trembling.
Oh, you weren't there.
How could you possibly....?


But the stone was gone, I tell you!
And there, all parcelled up, were the clothes,
So neat, catching the light;
And a smell of life in the tomb,
Keeping death at bay.


You know - but how could you? -
My heart spun upwards
As I saw the angel wink
And smile and disappear.
No, I can't prove it; but if
You'd felt my heart
Burst with a strange joy -
But then how could you possibly....?

## COLLEGE CHAPEL

Into the chapel clean and quiet,
Past the canary portals;
Take a sniff of the holy air -
'Tis bliss to sinful mortals.


Climb the hollow benefactions
On to a smooth trouser-pressed seat;
Cup your nose in your nice clean hands,
And pray - making sure your tie's still neat.


Change your penitent attitude:
Sneak a glance at your shoes, brand new.
Hold your talented head in your hands,
And pray - feeling if your parting's true.


How nice, o God, to be here in church -
But about time they got the heaters working.
At least things were hot for the early Christians.


All is vanity, saith the preacher,
All are equal in God's sight:
Why then fuss and preen and worry,
If only the heart is clean and white?
Got caught by the Dean
For not wearing a wedding garment tonight.

## THE PRODIGAL

I am the prodigal:
Not for me the constraints of home.
I am exploring the edges of my youth,
Forgetful of the myriad miles I've come.
I've thrown off the dull smock of obedience,
And put on golden attire;
Taking my senses out of the cupboard
I hold them over the fire.

My friends and my wealth give me pinions
As I soar ever nearer the sun.
How terrible the scorching of my soul
As the feathers melt away one by one.
And I spiral down into pig-swill
And tatters and jagged pieces of skin -
And a sigh from somewhere forgotten says:
"I will go home and be a servant of my kin."

\*\*\*\*\*\*\*\*\*\*\*\*\*\*\*\*\*\*

I am the elder brother
Controlling tightly my desire:
My dutiful eyes plead silently
For any sign of favour from my sire.
I did not ask all, risk all, lose all
As did my feckless younger brother.
Why then does my father not bestow on me
That special smile kept always for the other?

Now he is home again, and I grow cold;
Not for me the banqueting and joy.
I have grown older, more responsible - a man:
My father welcomes home his little boy.
Perhaps.... if only I could be a child again,
Peel off the layers of convention and the years,
And feel once more the love that duty killed -
Then might I too shed warm forgiving tears.

******************

I am the father of the prodigal:
My heart is torn in two.
I love both sons with equal fierceness,
Not for what they do,
But because they are mine, and need me,
And I created them for what they are.
That is why departure and rejection,
And abiding sullenness, leave an equal scar.

My tent of love is sorely stretched to cover them
When they are so far apart.
But if each in his own way will return,
I will give to each his portion of my heart.

# THE OUTSIDER

The tiger above, the pit below,
I cling to a rotting tree;
A mouse is nibbling at its roots:
Lord here am I, save me.


Tiger, tiger, burnished bright
With stripes of fire and pain:
The teeth of death gleam ivory white,
The devil holds the rein.


The pit is dark, I cannot see,
But I can smell its smell:
Death and oblivion grope around
That blackest nightmare well.


My fingers clutch the withered branch,
Its leaves with honey spread.
But I can see the gnawing mouse -
My lips are sealed with dread.


What, Lord, you too? A rotting tree?
And nailed to it, not clinging?
If you have been this way before
Then I'll endure it singing.

## THE PASSING

I am beyond the rainbow now,
My song is higher than the lark;
My refuge warmer than the womb,
My footfall softer than the dark.


My food is sweet as honeycomb,
My rest more peaceful than the grave,
My heart is light as thistledown;
And I am free as ocean wave.


I am enfolded in the arms
Of one who promised, on the tree:
"There is prepared for you today
A place in paradise with me".


So do not mourn for me, my friends:
The wind will dry the tears you spill.
My love still reaches out to you -
It has not changed, it never will.

# ST.DAVIDS

A thousand million buttercups
Were set on fire by the sun,
As I walked out to St.Davids Head -
So proud with my only son.


We talked at first of trivial things;
And then began to discourse
Of God and good and evil,
And which was the greater force.


His keen defence of the Devil
Was simple to confound:
For I had God and experience
And fought on familiar ground.


He accepted defeat and skipped ahead
As we turned inland from the bay;
In a harmony of silence
We walked the rest of the way.


Today I walk the cliffs alone.
The buttercups glimmer still;
And I turn the arguments over
And steel my unruly will -
While my son lies in a soldier's grave
At the foot of a foreign hill.

# OUT OF THE DEEP

Are you listening, Lord?
Are you there at all?
I know I'm insignificant;
I know I'm very small.

But my needs are a galaxy,
A cosmos my pain.
It consumes me utterly –
I'm wrapped in its train.

Will you help me, Lord?
You were once like me:
A man on a planet,
Confined in mortality.

Yet you won the battle, Lord,
By your steadfast love
You reached the stars again
With power from above.

Give me that power, Lord:
Let me not pray in vain.
Reach down and touch me:
Restore my soul again.

## THE NURSING HOME

"Dear Lord, what can I do,
Bedridden as I am and old and grey?
How can I serve my family and friends?"

"You can still pray."

"Cooped up in this small room,
Infirmity and nurses everywhere,
How can I be of any further use?"

"You can still care".

"Just waiting for my call,
Longing to be with loved ones up above,
What can I do to while away the time?"

"You can still love."

"How can I pray, care, love?
"My energies have long since ebbed away.

"Fix your eyes on Jesus, put your hand in his –
He'll show the way."

# THE SEVEN LAST WORDS FROM THE CROSS

## Father forgive them, they know not what they do:

They don't even love each other,
How can they possibly love you?
Each to himself hugs his own soul,
Each single-mindedly pursues his own goal,
Morality is convenience, not to be imposed,
Evil is not reality, merely supposed.
Every man is an island, in a barren sea:
I could walk upon their water,
If they would turn to me.


## Today thou shalt be with me in paradise.

Whatever the terrible deeds you have done,
The evil you have wrought upon mother and son,
The feeble conscience you have trampled down,
The lack of all compassion you have shown,
The self-loathing with which you have to deal,
The internal wounds that no one else can heal,
The physical agony upon you today
As your life ebbs inevitably, painfully, away -

All these bitter elements of the past
Are transformed by your faith at the last:
I love to hear such words of belief -
They help to assuage my own bitter grief.
Yes, this is why I hang here alongside you -
For you, my son, and all other sinners too.
Look at me if you can, amid the heaving and sighs.
Can you see the promise in my eyes?
Today thou shalt be with me in paradise.

**Son behold thy mother, mother behold thy son.**

Though I am on earth as the Son of God above,
In my life I have been nurtured by human love:
Love is the link that binds us everyone,
Father to daughter, mother to son,
Man to woman, brother to brother,
With ties that outweigh and outlast any other.
Those who laugh with us and with us weep
Are more than priceless rubies' worth to keep.

And so I thank you father for such love to me
Given by Joseph and my mother Mary,
And for the sweet companionship of John.
They must look to each other now that I am gone.
And may the Father's spirit of eternal love
Bring them at last to the blessed realms above.


**My God, my God, why hast thou forsaken me?**

You were there at my birth:  no question of that -
When the angels sang, and the shepherds sat
And the wise men knelt, at the door of the fold
And presented their gifts:  myrrh, frankincense, gold.
You were there at my birth.

You were there at my baptism, I knew in my heart
When cousin John, the one you set apart,
Looked hard at me amid the Jordan's flow
And said "It should be me", and I said "no -
Let it be this way, it is my Father's will".
And the dove hovered above us, almost still,
And we all heard your words.
I knew then, and remember now:
You were there at my baptism.

You were there at my trial in the desert, I knew.
When Satan sought to seduce me, and frustrate you.
It was your strength, your spirit, your word
Sharper than any two-edged sword -
That helped me endure those terrible days,
When I was tempted in so many ways
To seek human glory through superhuman power:
But you helped me remember
That this was not your purpose nor yet my hour.
You were there at my tempting.

You were there, Father, in the Garden last night.
How else could I have prevailed in such a fight?
I was striving to bind you, to appeal
For escape, for death, anything save this ordeal.
You saw the sweat, the blood, the final victory of your will
That has led me through the trial,
The scourging and derision, to this hill.
You were there with me in the Garden.

But, my beloved father, where are you now?
I need your presence, my dying is too slow.
Block out the sun, let the world not see
This final terrible obedient agony.
My God, my God, why hast thou forsaken me?

## I thirst

My first miracle torments me,
When I turned the water into wine.
I can taste that wine now, what freshness!
I crave that wine, that water, now.
If only the power were still mine.

And when I stood by the well
The woman came, and our eyes met;
And I told her of the water of life
And she went on her way rejoicing,
Her burden of past misdoings lifted.
Her gratitude haunts me yet.

And when I walked on the water
And dear impulsive Peter tried, and failed,
The air was so fresh, I was Lord of the elements,
I could command salt water, fresh water -
What power was mine, o Father.

And when I blessed the wine last night,
Among my trusted friends,
I could have drunk it all, downed it all,
Against this present cruel thirst
Had I but known.....

I knew I must suffer, my Father,
I knew I must come to this cross,
I knew I must undergo the torture,
The crown of thorns, the mockery of the trial,
But must I endure this dryness,
This unexpected burden,
This reminder of my humanity?
Aaaahhh! I thirst.

## It is finished

It is finished, the awesome task I came to do,
To reach out and bring back mankind to you.
And weary, torn and stricken though I am
To your purpose, in your strength, I have been true.
I can rejoice, I have put into reverse
The death-deserving flow of Adam's curse.

It is finished, it is over, it is done!
The task so monumental that the sun
Was dipped in blackest ink lest men should see
The writhing of their God in agony.
And now I rest, the dreadful price is paid,
Sheared are the evil puppet-master's strings,
And ransomed, pardoned, joined again with you
Are the poor foolish creatures you have made.

It is finished! Tetelestai!  At an end!
The bargain has been struck.  The price is paid.
And we have opened heaven to the sight
Of all the people in the world you made,
Whose sins withheld their spirits from your love
And made them Satan's puppets, by their will.
If only they believe this day's events,
There is hope, there is heaven for them still.

## Into thy hands I commend my Spirit

I am spent, dear father, I am spent.
Take my wilting spirit,
Fold me to your bosom,
Caress me with your hands of love,
Fill me once more with your strength,
Let me not dwell in the house of the dead.

I have conquered, dear father, I have won,
Smile upon me,
Show me signs of your pleasure,
Look again into my face,
Revive my soul,
Let me sit again with you on your throne.

I am dying, dear father, my eyes fail,
I am in the tunnel,
Hold on to me,
My heart is faint,
I travel the path of all flesh
In this human body.
Into thy hands I commend my spirit.

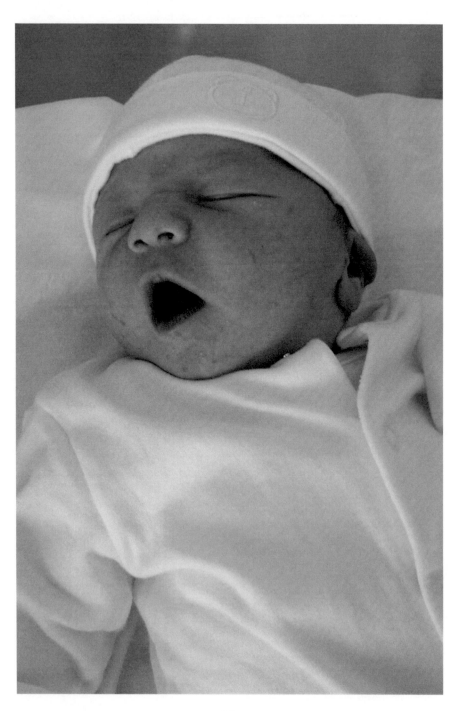

## WISE MAN'S HOMAGE

So there he was, a babe like any other,
Striving towards the nipple of his mother,
The tiny fingers waving in the air,
The nails as thin as paper, and the hair
So fine and downy, covering the head,
Blown by the draughts that wafted through the shed.

I felt the pulse beat in the fontanel,
I smelt that unique new-born baby smell,
I heard the little snuffling breaths and sighs,
I looked into those perfect sightless eyes.
Such impotence and weakness: could so frail
A human creature for mankind avail?

But then, this is the miracle of birth:
That every man who ever ruled the earth
Was once a baby, half an inch from death,
The slightest accident could snuff its breath.

Why then this babe? Why should I feel a stir
Of sadness, as I gave to him the myrrh?
The star had led me to this humble place,
But had not warned me what I was to face:
A king? A priest? For men to raise on high?
A death? God led me, but did not say why.

I knelt and paid my homage to the child,
Then rose and took my leave, no longer wise,
But much perturbed, with fancies running wild:
My answers lay no longer in the skies.
And yet I knew, 'mid all the mystery:
This helpless infant had been born for me.

# AT CHURCH

Why have you come to church today?
Is it an inward peace you desire?
A respite from all the daily strife
And noise of an over-busy life,
Traffic and kids and the tumble drier?

Or are you sunk in consuming sin?
Needing confession, forgiveness too?
Or wrestling with thoughts of revenge and hate
Against unjust treatment and unfair fate:
Perhaps the one to forgive is you?

Maybe you're here as it's Sunday today,
And you always come, and you're not sure why;
And you're full of doubts, and you're in a rut,
And your clothes are clean and your mind is shut,
And you're hoping there's Something after you die.

Perhaps you're glad and your heart is light,
You've passed your exams or you're deep in love,
And you want a chance to express your praise,
And thank the Lord for such happy days,
And join with angelic praise above.

Or are you burdened with grief and care?
You've lost a loved one, a friend is ill:
You need support, and a hand in yours,
As you struggle across to calmer shores,
Or toil up a never-ending hill.

Why are *you* here in church today?
Whatever the reason, be assured
That a meeting with Jesus will help you share
Your grief, your happiness, all your care.
So together let's come to our loving Lord.

# LAZARUS

My name is Lazarus:  I was dead for years.
My sisters prayed for me with many tears,
And when the Master listened to their plea,
He came and asked for me.

And everybody said "You're far too late.
You cannot help, it's been too long a wait."
And Jesus asked again:  "Where does he lie?
The gift of life have I."

Weeping, the sisters led him to my grave;
Jesus was weeping too, outside the cave.
I heard him pray, and then he gave a shout:
"Lazarus, come out!"

Bound as I was, entirely without sight,
I staggered from my grave into the light.
My friends unbound me, and I stood there free –
And could my saviour see.

My friend, the Master could do this for you,
Unlock your bonds, and give you vision too.
Raise you to life, and hold you as his own.
However dead you've grown.